JKJC

OUR GOVERNMENT

The Senate

by Mari Schuh

BELLWETHER MEDIA • MINNEAPOLIS, MN

Blastoff! Readers are carefully developed by literacy experts to build reading stamina and move students toward fluency by combining standards-based content with developmentally appropriate text.

LEVELS

Level 1 provides the most support through repetition of high-frequency words, light text, predictable sentence patterns, and strong visual support.

Level 2 offers early readers a bit more challenge through varied sentences, increased text load, and text-supportive special features.

Level 3 advances early-fluent readers toward fluency through increased text load, less reliance on photos, advancing concepts, longer sentences, and more complex special features.

★ **Blastoff! Universe**

Reading Level

Grade **K**

Grades **1–3**

Grade **4**

This edition first published in 2021 by Bellwether Media, Inc.

No part of this publication may be reproduced in whole or in part without written permission of the publisher. For information regarding permission, write to Bellwether Media, Inc., Attention: Permissions Department, 6012 Blue Circle Drive, Minnetonka, MN 55343.

Library of Congress Cataloging-in-Publication Data

Names: Schuh, Mari C., 1975- author.
Title: The Senate / by Mari Schuh.
Description: Minneapolis, MN : Bellwether Media, 2021. | Series: Blastoff! readers. Our government | Includes bibliographical references and index. | Audience: Ages 5-8 | Audience: Grades K-1 | Summary: "Developed by literacy experts for students in kindergarten through grade three, this book introduces the Senate to young readers through leveled text and related photos"–Provided by publisher.
Identifiers: LCCN 2019059252 (print) | LCCN 2019059253 (ebook) | ISBN 9781644872048 (library binding) | ISBN 9781681038285 (paperback) | ISBN 9781618919625 (ebook)
Subjects: LCSH: United States. Congress. Senate–Juvenile literature.
Classification: LCC JK1276 .S349 2021 (print) | LCC JK1276 (ebook) | DDC 328.73/071–dc23
LC record available at https://lccn.loc.gov/2019059252
LC ebook record available at https://lccn.loc.gov/2019059253

Editor: Rebecca Sabelko   Designer: Laura Sowers

Printed in the United States of America, North Mankato, MN.

Table of **Contents**

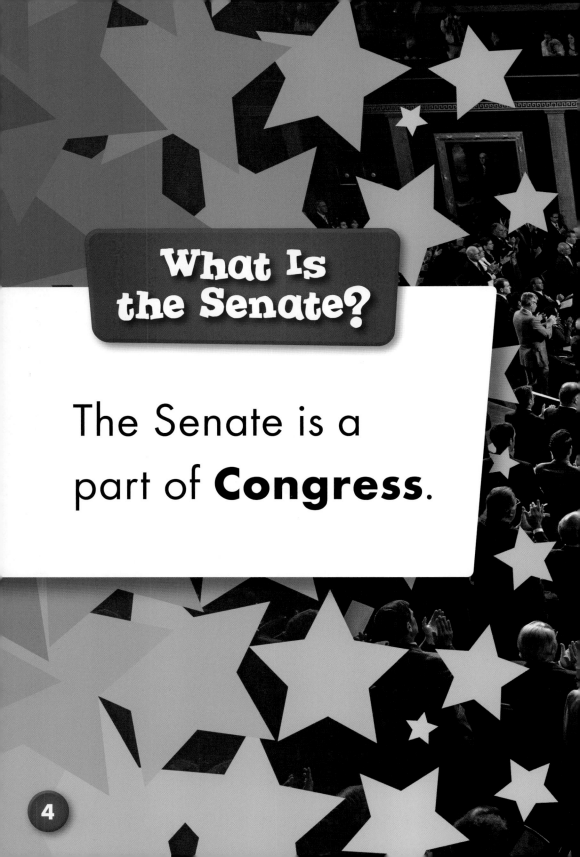

What Is the Senate?

The Senate is a part of **Congress**.

meeting of Congress

There are
100 **senators**.
The vice president
is the leader.

Working Together

Legislative Branch	Executive Branch	Judicial Branch
writes laws	signs laws	studies laws

president

vice president

Senate   House of Representatives

Supreme Court

Senators work
for their states.
Each state **elects** two.

Michigan senator Debbie Stabenow

Michigan senator Gary Peters

Must Haves

✓ 30 or older

✓ citizen for nine years or more

✓ lives in their state

Senators serve for six years. But they can serve again.

Senator
Tammy Duckworth

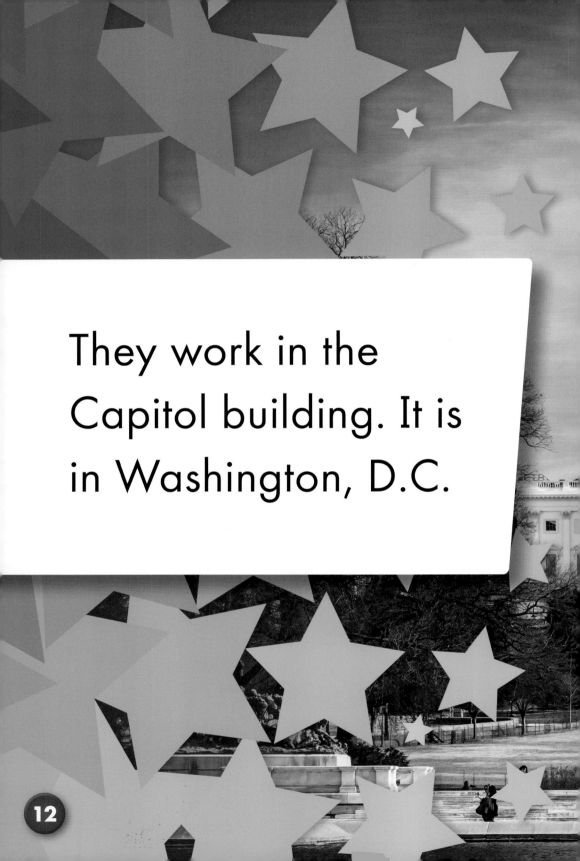

They work in the Capitol building. It is in Washington, D.C.

Capitol building,
Washington, D.C.

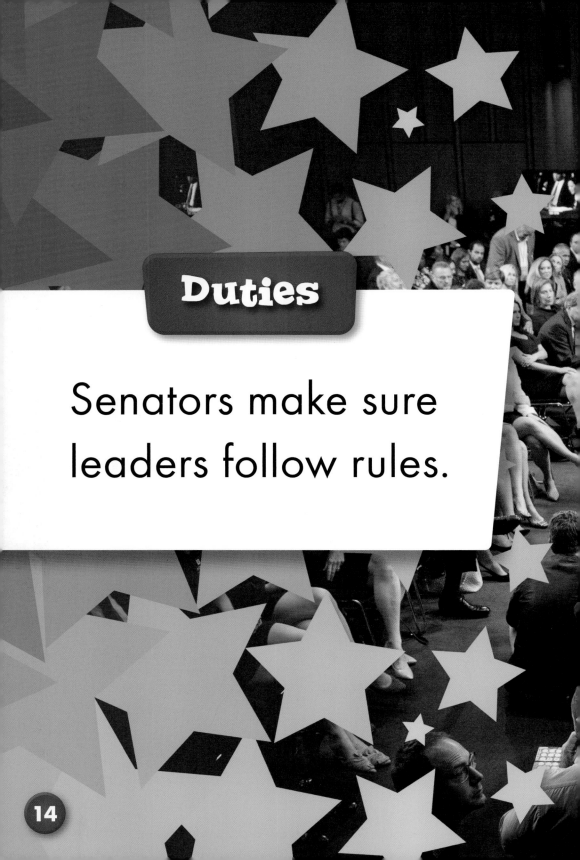

Duties

Senators make sure leaders follow rules.

They also write **bills**.
Some bills
become **laws**.

Senator
Chuck Schumer

Senators work together. They also meet with leaders.

Senator
Chris Van Hollen

Senator
Ben Cardin

UNITED STATES OF AMERICA

Senator
Carl Levin

Senator
Barbara Mikulski

19

Senators speak with **citizens**. They help people in their states!

If I Were a Senator...

What bills would I write?

Senator Elizabeth Warren

Glossary

bills

written ideas for new laws

elects

votes for someone to be a leader

citizens

members of a country

laws

rules that people must follow

Congress

the part of the government that makes laws

senators

members of the Senate; there are 100 United States senators.

To Learn More

AT THE LIBRARY
Bowers, Matt. *Understanding How Laws Are Made: American Government.* Mankato, Minn.: Amicus, 2020.

Rustad, Martha E. H. *U.S. Senate.* North Mankato, Minn.: Pebble, 2020.

Schuh, Mari. *The United States Constitution.* Minneapolis, Minn.: Bellwether Media, 2019.

ON THE WEB

FACTSURFER

Factsurfer.com gives you a safe, fun way to find more information.

1. Go to www.factsurfer.com.

2. Enter "Senate" into the search box and click 🔍.

3. Select your book cover to see a list of related content.

Index